I'm
NOT
Who
I
Was

LEAH SHORT

I'm Not Who I Was

by Leah Short

Copyright

United States Copyright Office

© 2014, I'm Not Who I Was
Leah Short
blessingscafe316@yahoo.com

ISBN-13: 978-0615975672

ISBN-10: 0615975674

**This book is dedicated
To my Children**

Rebecca, Erick, Caitie, Tyler and Joshua ❧

Acknowledgments

I want to first thank God for never giving up on me and Robert Paredes for believing in me.

Table of Contents

Introduction

From witchcraft to the pulpit, Leah Short tells her story of overcoming the devils and the strongmen that once held her family and her mind in captivity. In her captivating story, Leah details her struggles with molestation, drug addiction and hopelessness.

Find out how a woman who was once written off as a lost soul with no hope, found her way back to CHRIST.

ᚹChapter 1: The Beginning

Many years ago, Mercy Short was used as an
example by Cotton Mather. Mercy said he
loved God, but Cotton was going to prove
otherwise. Cotton was a Puritan minister and
the Puritan religion fueled witchcraft beliefs. No
one could understand the events of the
witchcraft crisis without an understanding of
the major role religion played in the lives of all
involved. Documents still exist from the time of
the trials that can provide insight into the period
spoke of in "A Brand Plucked out of the
Burning" by Cotton Mather.

Mercy was the victim of a terribly traumatic
series of events in 1690. The Short home was
raided by Native Americans, several family

members were murdered in front of her, and she was taken captive. Enduring such a brutal experience would no doubt have lasting effects. She was tortured by various "cursed specters". They gave her cruel pinches, stuck her with pins and subjected her to extreme fasting. In Mercy's mind, the devil was emblematic of the type of person who had brought her prior trauma. In Mercy's mind, the pain and fasting was similar to the pain she endured while she was in captivity. In addition, the experience that may have led Mercy to the state may have provided her with a way to externalized and displace feelings of anger through a psychological method called projection. In Mercy's case, a different type of psychological projecting may have occurred. Mercy may have felt anger and betrayal towards God for allowing her to experience such tragedy. Mercy knew that having such feelings against God would have been too distressing for anyone raised in a Puritan community. As a result, Mercy appeared to project her feelings onto an imagined devil. To others, she appeared to be having an argument with her invisible tormentor. She argued with her tormentor and could be heard saying, "Are you God? No? Then be gone, you devil!" The devil seemed to trick her into thinking he was God, so she was able to curse the devil and swear at God. She would say things like, "If you are Christ, I am sure you are a very odious one" and "You are not Christ! No! You are a beast." She used many offensive words against him calling him a "horrid wretch" and saying that hogs are the fittest company for him. Her outbursts appeared to be directed at the devil, but they also allowed her to curse God without appearing blasphemous. She would express anger about the tortures that she believed the devil and God had allowed her to go through. She would often say, "You pretend to show love for me. If you love me so much, then pray for me. Why do you starve me?" Mercy felt that God betrayed her. Because she could not express her anger towards God outright, she would project it onto the devil. Mercy seemed to question her belief in the Puritan religion. For example, when Cotton Mather was preaching, she flew upon him and tore a page of his Bible. Her actions may have been caused by the anger she felt towards a religion she felt was not providing her with protection against her misfortunes. While such behavior would not have been permitted under normal circumstances, her affliction allowed her to engage in such behavior without blame.

Cotton Mather felt that the fear of religion was beginning to decline. Along with other ministers, he used the witchcraft trials as a form for rejuvenating beliefs. He addressed the reader by stating, "If though had a desire to have seen hell, then look at Mercy Short. Here is one lying in outer darkness, haunted with the devil and his angels." He presented the case of Mercy Short as an example of the kind of suffering others would endure if they did not repent, painting a terrifying picture of the power of evil. Mercy's case also had a theological basis, and this lends further understanding to her actions. Her misfortunes caused her to question her faith in God, but the strict Puritan culture would have made it impossible for Mercy to express her feelings outright. As a result, her affliction seemed to validate the religious beliefs of others. Many believed that her religious uncertainly caused her to exhibit blasphemous outbursts. My family took this story, ran with it and started to worship the devil, practicing witchcraft.

Mark 5:9-13- Then Jesus asked him, "What is

your name?"

"My name is Legion," he replied, "for we are many." And he begged Jesus again and again not to send them out of the area. A large herd of pigs was feeding on the nearby hillside. The demons begged Jesus, "Send us among the pigs; allow us to go into them." He gave them permission, and the impure spirits came out and went into the pigs. The herd, about two thousand in number, rushed down the steep bank into the lake and were drowned.

ᔕ◦Chapter 2: Lost and of the World

My father was born in Coleman, Texas in 1937.
He was born to a mother who came to the
United States from Germany. His mother had
once been held captive by one of the most evil
men in history: Hitler. Hitler was just like Cotton
Mather and my grandmother was like Mercy.
She had been put in a prison that she would
escape; nevertheless, she never escaped the
tormenting prison in her mind. My
grandmother would often sleep in a small
space in her closet. She would also sit at the
table for hours, drinking coffee and chain
smoking cigarettes. When we would sit and
talk with her, we would often catch a glimpse of
the numbers on her arm from the days of her

torments. She would not talk about those days, however. My grandfather was full blooded Indian, and he was a very kind soul. All I remember about him is that he would make us purses and shoes from leather.

My father grew up like any normal all-American boy in the 40's and 50's. He would marry his first wife Margie, and have a daughter by the name of Debbie Lee. He joined the Army and then met my mother. At that time, my mother was pregnant with my half-sister Torrie. He would go on to marry my mother, even though he was still married to his first wife. My mother did not know until the day the military police showed up at the door and put my father under arrest. They were going to court marshal my father for bigamy, but by only the grace of God, he was not charged. A year later, my sister Babette was born. Babette was a child who always seemed to be mad at the world. I always told my mother that she did not bond with her. My mother even joked that she thought Babette was retarded. I was born two years later, then my brother Robert Jr.

At the age of three, I was molested by a family friend. As I grew up, I would often wonder who the man was and what he was doing to me. My father would do what he could to make a living. I remember there was always different cars at our house. I would find out later that they were stolen cars. Additionally, my father loved to smoke marijuana. Years later, my father introduced us to witchcraft and drugs. I was only twelve years old at that time. He called it white magic so we all thought it was okay since it was not called black magic; nevertheless, it was all the same. My father owned several books on spells, and we would often go to the occult shop that was located on Yale Street. There, we would purchase all kinds of herb candles and various items to practice witchcraft.

In one peculiar incident, I had bought a sword for my father at the occult shop, and we had gone back about two weeks later to get a few things. When we arrived there, were told there was no way we had bought the sword there because the owner had passed away three months prior to our visit. That was the last time I would go to the occult shop for next ten years; nevertheless, over the years, I continued to walk with the dark side. My friend Helen and I would often play with the Ouija board and open up portals into the demonic, and bad things would happen to people who'd done us wrong. In my mind, I thought it was so awesome that Satan would do what we wished on other people.

One day, my father was busted for selling

drugs after the DEA stopped him on the I-10 freeway. There were no drugs in the car so they took him back to our house. They didn't have a warrant so they told him that they would take my niece Candice to Child Protective Services if he did not show them where the drugs were. He did and he was arrested and taken to the south side jail. We could not find him for three days. He had to go before a judge by the name of Pat. She asked him when the last time he had used drugs was, and he told her that the last time he'd used was when he was arrested. The judge sent him for drug testing and he tested positive. Consequentially, the judge charged him with contempt of court and sent him to the county jail for thirty days. While he was locked up, the Cuban Mafia tried to kidnap my brother to keep my dad from telling who he was dealing drugs for. He was not going to give that information to the DEA. After all that happened, my family became divided, eventually going our own ways.

In 1984, I met Colin. I was sixteen years old and my father did not like him. At that time, we were living in southwest Houston and I would secretly steal away to meet Colin at a local park. My Dad found out and put me out of the house.

I stayed in Colin's car because I had nowhere to go. I felt hopeless knocking on strangers' doors to use the restroom. I did not know when I would eat again and I would often go two to three days without eating. Colin and I would do drugs and hang out wherever we could. My sister Babette and I would watch this drug dealer's house. The drug dealer had meth labs all over, so we had it good, doing drugs and living the high life. All we had to do was pay his bills for him when he was not there, but one day, he had come to the house and put us out. He would not give us our clothes so we were back on the street without a thing. At that time, I became pregnant with Rebecca and while I was pregnant, I did not do drugs.

Colin and I had a lot of problems. I was seventeen years old, but forced to grow up fast. While still on the streets, I had gone to Colin's house where he lived with his father. I was very sick while pregnant with Rebecca. I asked Colin's father if I could use his restroom because I was feeling sick. His dad asked me if I was pregnant and when I confirmed that I was, he gave me a place to live. Later on, we found a place of our own next to a meth lab.

Colin was an abusive man. He would often fight with me and he would tell me that I was having a demon seed.

Rebecca was born in September of 1985, and she was a good baby. One day I came home and found that Colin had put Rebecca in one of our closets because he did not want to hear her cry, and this enraged me. Because of that incident, one day while he was at work, I moved and took everything with me. I did not want Rebecca to go through that kind of abuse, even though I was doing drugs and my life was a total mess.

I met Glenn in 1987, and I married him three months after I met him. The day of our marriage took a bad turn when he got drunk and grabbed me by my arms, causing them to bruise. For the next eight years, he would hit and choke me. We would stay at vacant houses doing drugs and going to hotels to smoke cocaine. Later on, I would give birth to three boys: Erick, Tyler and Joshua, and my daughter, Caitlian.

For the first two years of our life together, Glenn and I would get high every day. We would snort or smoke cocaine, and we destroyed many lives with our reckless ways. What's amazing is I did not do drugs while I was pregnant with Rebecca or Erick, but after I gave birth, I would start to get high again. My life was out of control. I was doing cocaine every day and nothing else mattered but getting high. Glenn would go out and steal so we could get high. As I think back, I just could not believe this was my life and what I had become. My son Erick and I did not bond because of my drug abuse. When he was a baby, my sister in law took him in and I asked her if she wanted to adopt him. Because of that, I have so much regret in my heart. If I was not living for the world and having the influences of the devil, I would never have given up one of my children.

I remember when the show Cops had just came out. Around that time, I would get so high, I would become paranoid. One day after getting high, the paranoia set in so bad that I just got down on my knees and poured out to God. I said to Him, "I can't live like this anymore," and that day I was delivered from drugs. The amazing part is I wasn't saved yet. That happened in 1989, and five years later, I gave my life to Christ at Brownsville Assembly of God, in Pensacola, Florida. That church was pastored by John Kilpatrick.

Before we left Texas, Glenn tried to rape me. I called the police and his sister told him to go to bed. She told him that we were leaving the next day to start a new life. I should have walked away that night, but God had a plan for my life.

Life seemed good until Glenn started to drink

again. In April of 1995, Glenn went to jail for hitting my son Tyler. Child Protective Services came out to the house to see if he had abused any of my other children, and Rebecca told the CPS worker that Glenn had molested her. A police officer went to Glenn's place of employment and spoke to him about her accusations. Glenn called me on the phone and told me he was on his way to chop my head off. I was going to shoot him if he came because one of my friends had given me a shotgun to protect myself. I was not sure what he was capable of doing and where his mind was at. I was tired and I did not want to be his victim anymore, and thankfully, he never showed up. Then he called and asked if I would take him to turn himself in so I drove him to the police station. I knew this was my way out of the hell that I was living in. Two days later, I took off for Texas and I never looked back.

About two months later, the District Attorney called me and stated they were going to offer him a thirteen year prison sentence. I was so pleased with the sentence because he had to sit still and think about what he had done to my little girl. I was happy when he took the offer.

Meanwhile, I was trying to raise four children by myself. Glenn's family came to Houston and told me there was no way to get a divorce. They claimed that Glenn was falsely accused because I wanted out of our marriage. Who would do this to someone? Glenn's parents told me they would take Tyler and Caitie until I got on my feet. I was dating many men just trying to be loved.

Then I met Robert and I wanted to make a life with him, so we bought a four bedroom house. One day, Glenn's parents called and asked if they could speak with my daughter Rebecca, and I agreed. At that time, Rebecca was locked up at Texas youth commission for stealing a car. Glenn's parents wanted her to tell the court that she'd lied about the molestation so Glenn would not come out of prison as a sex offender. Rebecca told them that should would not lie. She reminded them that she was ten years old when he molested her and he had no right to do that to her. We had my children for two weeks and I had to take Erick back because Diane had adopted him, but when I arrived back in Florida, I found out they had adopted Caitie and Tyler as well. They'd told the judge that they did not know where I was, so he granted them the adoption. I was so hurt that I cried all the way back to Texas. How could this happen? Because of this incident, I walked away from God. I questioned how God could allow this to happen to me. I was angry with God. I wanted my life back and I wanted my children back. I did not realize it at that time, but that's how the devil works. He is here to kill, steal and to destroy. He was so angry with me for no longer walking hand in hand with him. The only way he could truly attack me was through my children. My heart was so heavy for the next few years that I cried often.

Rebecca was so messed up over everything Glenn did to her that she became a cutter. She would later claim to be Wiccan and was walking with Satan. The last time I saw Erick and Tyler was in 2002. Tyler once told me that the Bible says you should honor your mother and father, but I was not his mother. That was a dagger that struck me through my heart. Erick is so angry, he will not even talk to me; nevertheless, the devil has not won.

In 1995, I was living with a friend that I grew up with named Tarri, and one day, we were on a chat line scamming men. We did whatever we wanted to live the high life, but I was lonely, so I called out to God and asked Him to give me a man that was not like any of the men I've had in my life. Not long after that, I met a man named Robert. I was in awe, and I felt like God had answered my prayers. Life was good for the next seven years, or so I thought. In 2002, Robert and I moved to Tucson, Arizona and that's when Robert started to change. He started coming home late. I wanted to find out why he'd changed, so I hacked into his email and found out that he was seeing another woman. That's when my world came crashing down around me. I spent the next five years so angry with him that I began to hate him. At night while he was asleep, I would think of ways to kill him and get away with the crime. I was so depressed and angry. How could this man betray me like that after I'd done everything I could for him? He was my world.

ᏽ♠Chapter 3: Saved By Grace

In 2007, I started telling myself that I could not
live the way I was living anymore. I could no
longer live with all the betrayal. I told Robert
that I could no longer live the way we were
living. My joy was gone and I felt as if I was
drowning and we were going our separate
ways. I told him that he had until the first of
August to decide if he would be keeping the
house or if he would be leaving. My son,
Joshua went to church with one of the
lifeguards from the public pool and then he
went to country camp for four days. In the
meantime, I checked Robert into a mental
hospital because he was wanting to kill himself.
He came home talking about a movie titled "A

Conversation with God." They'd played that movie at the mental hospital. I told him I wanted to go to church. I wanted to attend Believer's World Outreach Church, pastored by Tommy and Rachel Burchfield. He did not want to go because he wanted to go to the Catholic Church. I told him that he could go to the Catholic Church, but I was going to the church that was Spirit-filled. I wanted to go to a church that had bible based teaching; a church where there were signs, wonders and miracles that where happening. I wanted to be in midst of it all. God was calling me to Believer's World Outreach Church. Robert went to a catholic church, and I was so mad at him for not wanting to go experience God with me. The next week, he said agreed to come with me. During praise and worship, a man bumped Robert on the head, and I thought he was never going to come back to that church with me again, but he did. Later, we laughed and

24

joked that God hit him on the head and said, "Sit still and know I am God." Two months later, he was invited to go to a man's retreat by David Jones (now Pastor David Jones), so Robert got on the bus to country camp. He sat his first night in praise and worship and the next morning all the men went to the Prayer Garden, and Robert was called forth. A man named Mac asked him about being catholic, and right there, Robert received salvation.

Jeremiah 33:3- "Call unto me and I will answer you and tell you great and mighty things you do not know."

Robert was slain in the spirit. It took one touch of the Holy Spirit, and after that, Robert and I were so hungry for the word of God that we would be at church every time the doors were open.

My son Joshua was going to the country camp and life was good. We were in prayer before church service and God spoke to me about opening a cafe. He told me to name it "Blessings Cafe", so I went into prayer and said to God, "Okay, you want me to open the cafe. God, I ask you provide me what I need and I will do as you said." I found a location and it was fully stocked with what I needed. I was given the location with no money and the man that owned the location provided me with food for seven weeks.

I would work from the time it opened until the time it closed. Business was good.

One Wednesday afternoon, I was going to close the cafe early and take my employee to church with me. That employee had never been to church or knew God. A couple came in to eat, so I started a conversation with them. I told them about God and how He provided what I needed to start my cafe. The man I was speaking with said, "Wow, I know this is God. I want to step out on faith and start my company." I ministered to him and he stepped out in faith and was given some high end contacts. Next, a women came into the cafe looking distracted and wanting something to drink. My heart started pounding and that small still voice told me to pray for her. I had never prayed for anyone one-on-one, so I was scared. Josh was outside somewhere, so I went into the kitchen and cried out to God. I said to God, "Please send Josh here." Around that time, Josh rode up on a bike. I told Josh we needed to pray for this lady, and he agreed. Josh sat down with her and asked her, "Can we pray for you?" She responded with, "Who are you people? It does not matter. I am going to kill myself anyway." Josh ministered to her and she started crying and hugging him. I asked if we could call someone for her.

The sister we called sent the police and an ambulance, so she became angry. The officer told me she needed to go to the hospital, but she would not go unless Josh went with her so I agreed to let him go with her. When we arrived at the hospital, the doctor said if we had not came to the hospital, she would have died. Her sugar count was so high, it was not reading. God sent her our way so he could save her, and she would give her life to Christ. We stayed open for about three more weeks because the world was under a recession. Gas was high and people were not eating out much, so we closed the cafe.

In 2008, we were on our way to church and Josh told me that God had a word for him. I told him that even though I gave my life to Christ, I did not know what to do so he needed to talk to the pastor. After church service, Josh went down to the pastor, and I saw Josh fall to the ground and be slain in the Spirit. I saw some of the men sit him in a chair. One of the men said to me, "It looks like you are going to have to carry him to the car." Some of the men then carried him to the car. One of the elders of the church said to me, "I hope you have child lock on that car." I was worried that he would get out of car while I was driving. On the ride home, Josh was talking in a strange tongue. I was not sure what was going on because I had never seen or heard anything like that before. When we arrived home, we carried Josh into the house and placed him on the couch. He had been slain in the Spirit for almost two hours, and when he came back to earth, he was weeping and saying that Jesus had taken him to heaven and hell.

Joshua's Heaven experience: When the Lord blessed Josh with a vision of heaven and hell, he was slain in the Spirit and felt a sudden rush. He said that it felt like he was moving with incredible speed; like being shot out of a sling shot straight up in the air. Then, in a blink of an eye, he was standing on the most beautiful landscape he had ever seen. It was a landscape which was impossible to describe. The words "stunning" or "beautiful" couldn't even come close to what he was looking at. He saw mountains that looked like diamonds and other precious gems. And all the colors were enhanced. The best way he could describe the earth in comparison to heaven is by saying that the earth is a seventies tube television, and heaven is the new blue-ray television. The grass looked like a sea of emeralds and the sky looked like sapphire. He was in such awe that he realized he was holding his breath, but to him, the strange thing was he had no desire to breathe, even though he could breathe if he wanted to. Then, he heard a voice that sounded like a thousand trumpets being blown, calling his name. At that moment, he heard a voice that he recognized. The voice was that of Christ. He turned and fell to his face and worshiped his Lord Jesus Christ, and He told him to rise. Jesus had so much to show and tell him, so they started walking through heaven. The streets are really made of gold and the buildings and houses looked like they were made of pure pearls. The Lord told him that He was showing him this because he was going to be a light for this misguided generation. He also said, "Behold, for everything I am going to show you will not be glorious and awe. Some of it will be horrible and unimaginable, but keep faith and know I will be right beside you and everything I do, I do for a greater purpose and reason that I know will benefit the child of the most high God." So, after He tells him this, they walk and talk some more. Joshua saw angels, and the river of life that contained the souls of all the people who never had the chance to hear the gospel and know Jesus as their Lord and Savior. They are waiting for Judgment, the day when earth is destroyed and heaven will descend upon the earth. In the river, there are also aborted and miscarried babies waiting for the mothers.

Joshua's hell experience: After Jesus showed him heaven, they descended into hell, and what he saw was horrific. He saw a pit of people being tormented by demons, people being eaten by maggots and other types of bugs, and people being ripped apart limb by limb. In hell, you have all your senses. What's worse is that your senses are enhanced so your torment is worse both physically and emotionally. For example, he saw someone being skinned whole. When the demons were done, the woman's skin grew back, causing her even more pain. Everything just keeps

repeating itself over and over for all eternity.
There are no breaks and the feeling of despair
is overwhelming. And the smell of burning flesh
was magnified. The more evil you did on earth,
the worse your punishment will be. At the same
time, the feeling of being totally separated from
God is too overwhelming. Someone touched
Josh while he was in hell, and my son who was
a good boy turned to bad boy overnight.
I did not understand his sudden change since
he had a calling on his life. Four months later, a
guest speaker named Sammy Maloof who was
an actor and stuntman came to our church on
Good Friday of 2008. Joshua was crying during
worship, and I thought to myself that he was
feeling convicted for all the bad things he had
been doing. They had altar call at the end of
service, and Josh, along with two more
individuals went down to the altar. The music
was loud, so I could not hear what was being
said, but I saw my son fall. He was slain in the

Spirit. I then saw my son stand up as though one was standing him up by his underarms. I saw him fall forward, and I saw the pastor telling Josh something, so I went closer to hear. The pastor grabbed my hand and said to me, "Momma, you got to believe." Of course, I was scared. Then, I saw my son elevate about six inches off the ground and his eyes looked yellow. He was speaking demonic, and it took about an hour to deliver my son from Satan's hold. After that, we went home and the next day, Sammy was doing stunts in the parking lot of the church. We went to check him out, but I had to go to work. Later that evening, Robert called me and said he was standing in our closet. He said that he felt like he had just ran a mile and broke out in a sweat. He was scared and was going to come up to my job. When he arrived at my place of work, his hair was out of place and this was strange because his hair was never out of place. It struck me as odd, but we were busy so I sent a co-worker named Nelly to check on Robert. Nelly came back running and told me that Robert said in an evil voice, "Get away." I was not scared, so I walked up to him and asked, "Are you okay?" I took his cell phone from his hand, and he said to me in the same evil voice to get away from him. I looked at his phone and saw that he had sent a text to the pastor that read, "HE IS MINE." I called the pastor and told him what was going on, and he said he was on his way to where we were. Meanwhile, I called my other son, Josh, and he said to me, "Mom, I am not strong enough to fight the demon." I told him to come where we were anyway. In the meantime, I was yelling at the demon and telling it that it was going back to the pit of hell. I kept putting anointing oil on Robert. Josh arrived and I told Brittany to stay outside because she was a baby Christian. We were fighting the demon and some people from another church came and started praying. Then the police showed up and wanted to know if Robert was drunk or high on drugs. They had their tasers drawn, and I told them that he was demon possessed. Around that time, Pastor David Jones and Sammy Maloof arrived and took Robert and Josh away. The police asked me, "So, you have someone to call when these things happen?" I responded with, "Yes, it is called the church."

I was stuck at work until someone came to take over my shift. By the time I arrived at the church, Robert was delivered from the demonic spirit. They told me that the demon was jumping from Josh to Robert, and they were both covered in anointing oil.

Everything seemed okay until a year later when I received a call from Brittany's boyfriend saying that Brittany was acting funny. She was lying on the couch speaking in a demonic voice. He said that he would lay the bible on her, and she would throw it across the room. I told him I was about twenty minutes away; I would call Robert and Josh, and we would be there shortly. About five minutes later, he called again and said he got in the truck with the baby and locked the doors because Brittany had a knife and wanted her baby. Suddenly, the locks of the trucked popped up and Brittany was able to get in, so he said he was coming to us. I picked Josh up because he was at the movies. He told me God told him to fill up the bath tub, so we went into prayer for protection over us. Robert was slain in the Spirit, and Rebecca; my oldest child, was scared. All a sudden, the doorbell rang frantically. I couldn't believe someone would be at the door at that time. I opened the door and no one was there. I then realized a demon needed to flee because our house had a hedge of protection over it.

Brittany and Winfield showed up about ten minutes later. When Brittany walked in, I said to her, "Hey Brittany; what you doing?" She responded with, "I am not possessed." I told her that no one said she was possessed. I requested that we sit down and talk. All of a sudden, we saw her hands drop and her eyes rolled into the back of her head. Josh and Winfield picked her up and took her upstairs to put her in water. She was like a cat being put in water. Josh picked her up and placed her in the water, dunking her as she thrashed about. He dunked her about three more times, and when it was all done, she was back to her old self, smiling and laughing.

In 2010, Rebecca became pregnant and I was so happy that I was going to be a grandmother. Rebecca and I started to get everything for the new baby that was on the way. We even started picking out names for the baby. One day, Rebecca started to bleed, so we went to hospital, but they told her that everything was okay. I remember her saying, "I know God is not going to take this baby from me." About two weeks later, she lost the baby and when she went to the hospital, they threw her baby away like a piece of trash. She was so angry with God at that point that she went on a path of self-desecration. She was working and still going out, picking up men and robbing them.

On November 13th, Rebecca, Joshua and Brittany went shopping. Rebecca had just gotten a gaming system and they were going to get a new game. Somewhere along the way, they went to see one of her friends. A man walked up to Joshua and asked him if he wanted to buy one of the girls for twenty dollars. Joshua and the man got into a scuffle and Rebecca just lost it. She picked up a clothes iron and beat the man without mercy.

Joshua finally got her to stop, but not before stomping on his head. They took off running and the police eventually caught up with them and arrested them. I called them and there was no answer. At around eleven o'clock that evening, Joshua called me and told me that they were in jail and he told me where the car was. I found out that Brittany had run and had not been caught. The police released the car keys to me and asked me a few questions. I found out they were being charged with aggravated robbery with a deadly weapon. Rebecca took a plea of 10 years. Joshua's lawyer said he could get Joshua out on probation. We went before the judge and they asked me some things about my son. The judge refused to listen to what I had to say, and when I was finished speaking, they asked Joshua a few questions. After that, the judge sentenced him to twenty years in prison.

I turned to Robert and asked him if the judge had sentenced Joshua to twenty years, but Robert was not sure. Joshua turned to be led back to the holding cell, and I formed that very same question to Joshua with my lips. I silently lipped to him, "Twenty years?" He shook his head in affirmation. At that point, I lost it and some lady started hugging me and telling me everything was going to be alright. I went to the parking lot and broke down. I was so mad at God because I felt like God had lied to me. I had been getting a word that Joshua would come home. We went home and Robert had also began to lose his faith. In the midst of anger and grief, we saw that Jesse Duplantis had tweeted that he was in town. We took off to see him, and he preached about losing one's faith. After that, Robert was back on his game with God, praying and worshiping.

As for me, I was grieving like my son had been

put to death. I was lost and in so much pain that I could not bear getting out of bed. I didn't have joy in my life for two months. In my darkest hour, I would go to a service at Family Worship Center, pastored by Richard and Tina Ford. One of Pastor Ford's message was "Come Out, Come Out from wherever you are." I wept because I knew God was speaking to me to get up and fix my face. He was reminding me that He has given me joy and not sorrow. I was crying out to God and reminding Him that He said Joshua was going to preach His Word one day. He said, "Yes, but for now, he is going to preach from behind those prison walls. Those prison walls are full of the lost and broken." Suddenly, I was visiting Josh, separated by glass. I couldn't even hug my son. He was shackled, and I was crying because it hurt me to see him that way. My son said to me, "Stop crying, Mom. I am okay. God has me. I have favor." Every time I visit him, we have church.

One day (I believe it is in April 2012), we met
Brandon Barber, and we were hanging out with
him and getting ready to launch a church we
called Elevate Church. We signed up to do jail
ministry with them, going into the jails to
minister to the inmates. On my first visit at the
county jail, my nerves were in the pit of my gut.
I went to the chaplain's office and was told I
was going in by myself. I said to GOD, "What?
Oh, okay. God, you're funny. I do not know
what to do." God said, "Yes, you do. You have
the Holy Spirit within you."

I walked into the jail pod, and I was surprised
at what I saw. Girls were on their bunks taking
showers and talking on the phone. When they
realized I was there, they crowded around me
wanting the books that I had. I told them that if
they listened to what I had to say, they could

have the books. I then sat down at a table and I had ten women sitting with me. I had a message for them entitled "Freedom from Failure." As I was ministering to the women, they began weeping and my heart began to fill with joy. The Holy Spirit spoke to me about one of the girls. She had pale skin and dark hair. I told her to come sit by me and she did. I spoke with her, and she told me that no one had ever talked with her about Jesus. She had never even been to church. I spoke to her and asked her if she was ready to accept Jesus into her heart, and she was. All the women were crying with joy that she was giving her life to Christ. There was also a woman there who knew God and His Word. She had walked away from God, but was ready to give her life back to our Father. On my first visit, I had one salvation and nine rededications. I was on a Holy Ghost high.

Chapter 3: Saved by Grace

In January of 2013, I was on Facebook when I saw a post from a Pastor Vaughaligan Walwyn. He needed help launching his new church called Legacy. I contacted him and told him I would love to help him and he accepted my offer. As I walked into the church, God spoke to me and said to me, "You are home." I said to Robert, "This is where God wants us." He responded with, "What do you mean? I love Elevate Church." I told him we could go to both churches, but that was not God's plan. We were to give Legacy Church one hundred percent, so we became prayer partners. Eventually, we signed up for the prison ministry with a part of Legacy Church called Con-victory. Tracy Dudley called and asked me if Robert and I would go to the Pam Lyncher Unit. I was thrilled to go. We arrived at the prison, and was waiting in the lobby for the rest of the Legacy team. That's when a guard came and asked us if we were ready to go to the back. I told him I was told that we were waiting on others, and he told me that Robert and I were it. I leaned over and told Robert that we were to give the message.

We did not have anything planned, so I told Robert we were going to have what I referred to as testimony Sunday, and God moved in that place. We left that prison overwhelmed and happy that God would use us the way He did. It was to show the inmates that even though our children were serving ten and twenty year sentences, we were still serving God.

On May 25th, we had a deliverance with the Deleon family. We laid hands on Anna in our fireside room, and the Holy Spirit spoke to me. He told me we needed to go to their house, so we did. When we arrived, nothing seemed to be out of place, but when Robert and Joe started anointing the house, I heard Marisa yell my name. When I went to the bedroom, one of the girls was on all fours throwing up. It looked like a scene from the movie Exorcist. We grabbed the child, started praying and laying hands on her, casting that demon out of her. We didn't arrive home until around four in the morning. We were tired, but could not go to sleep because we had so much excitement from witnessing the power of God. The next day, we continued to pray and love on this family. At this time, I knew what my calling was. I was to be on a deliverance team. Months would pass and we started a bible study at the home of Richard and Joanna Vega. Bible study was so awesome. The Holy Spirit would show up and show off.

On July 30th, we had bible study, and Richard wanted more of God, so God showed up and showed off. After bible study, we would always pray for one another. Richard asked us to pray

for Alazae. When we were praying, Cidia and I
felt an evil spirit pass between us. Cidia
grabbed on to Robert, and started crying and
shaking her head. I told her everything was
alright. That's when Robert fell into the spirit
and fell to the floor, so we sat him on the
couch. Richard said to Alazae, "Do you see
that guy? He is battling for you." Richard then
told me that Alazae likes the Gothic lifestyle. I
asked her if she still wanted to be Gothic, and
she said yes. At that moment, I saw her chest
rise and her head twitch. I told Richard that we
needed to do deliverance immediately, and that
Joanna and I needed to lay hands on Alazae.
Joanna said to me, "I don't know what to do." I
told her the Holy Spirit would guide her. We
took Alazae to another room while the others
were anointing the other children. When we
took Alazae in the other room, the demon
spoke to me and told me it wanted to hurt me.
All I could think to say at that time was, "Okay.

Let's do this. Bring it on, Satan. I was ready to do whatever I had to do to save this child from Satan's hands. We started praying and laying hands on her and we could hear the demons screaming.

Alazae fell to the floor. Her feet were stiff and her toes were curled. By this time, Richard was in the room praying and then Robert came in and started praying and laying hands on the child. That's when I noticed Richard trying to call someone. I asked him, "Who are you calling? Now is not the time." He said, "I'm trying to call a friend to pray with us." I told him that the call was not going to go through because we were in the spirit realm, and all Richard heard was static on the phone. God told me fill up the bathtub.

I went and found Victor and told him to fill up the tub. At that time, Robert was alone with the demon, and he saw the face of Alazae transform into the demon. The demonic spirit was laughing as if to tell him that Alazae was his, and he would not deliver her from it. I took off Alazae's shoes and told everyone to move hastily; it was time to take her to the water. As they took her into the bathroom, she grabbed the sides of the door frame because she did not want to go in the water. Robert dunked Alazae, and we could see bubbles coming out of her nose. That night, my prayer language changed.

As we pulled Alazae out of the water, we could see the change in her. We left her with her father Richard to answer the questions that she had. We went downstairs and saw Victor crying, so we prayed for understanding to explain to him what he had just witnessed. I thank God I have The Holy Spirit to guide me and give me the wisdom to answer all the questions everyone had about the incident.

Jeremiah 29:11- "For I know the plans I have for you declared the Lord."

God has picked me up and placed my feet upon a Rock. I wrote this book to tell you if He can take this broken girl who once worshiped the Devil, He can use you.

If God can clean me up and use me to do His will, He can use you as well. It doesn't matter how hopeless or worthless you feel, God wants to be your heavenly Father. I am now in leadership in my church and a certified Life Coach. God is the way, the truth and the light. It doesn't matter how far in darkness you may be, God will clean you up and use you if you let Him.

Contact Information

If this book blessed you and you are searching for the touch of God, visit us at:

CT Legacy Church

9701 Almeda-Genoa Road

Houston, Texas 77075

You can also find me on Face book @ LeahshortPope.

I would love to bless you, love on you and speak life into you. Thank you and God bless you.